I Suwannee & Poems

Johnny Summerfield

Copyright © Johnny Summerfield, 2017
Copyright Cover Art © Adobe Stock Image *Cypress Swamp*, licensed 2017
Printed in the United States of America

All Rights Reserved

Library of Congress Control Number: 2017902696

ISBN: 978-0-9986857-4-8

First part of this manuscript originally published in 2007 as *I, Suwannee*

I Suwannee & Poems by Johnny Summerfield
Johnny Summerfield 1966 -

Published by Summerfield Publishing d.b.a. New Plains Press
PO Box 1946
Auburn, Alabama 36831-1946

newplainspress.com

email: publisher@newplainspress.com

"Dawn's" and "Rolling Stone" were previously published in *Arden*, a student, staff, and faculty journal of Columbus State University, Columbus, GA. The poem "Rolling Stone" has changed slightly since then.

Table of Contents

I Suwannee

History	13
A Poem in Bronte's *Agnes Grey and Poems*	17
Sustenance	18
Shallow	19
Contained	20
Homecoming	21
Crossing Place	22
Sailing it Off, Up the Suwannee	23
Down by the Riverside	24
Fountain of Youth	25
The Underground River	26
Day	27
Like Searching	28
The Shoals	29
Dawn's	30
Down	31
After the Rain	32
Deep Tone	33
Fixed	34
Tourists	35
An Old Bridge Pylon	36
The Live Oak	37
Bald Eagles	38
Formation	39

Out of Water	40
I Am Clay in a Kiln	42
Horses	43
Bird's Eye View	44
Metamorphosis	45
Off 136A	46
An Upside Down Umbrella	48
Degrees of Heat	49
River Caverns	50
Johnny Darter Planted in Leafy Mud	52
Locals	53
Movement	54
Summer Time	56
By Chance Viewing	57
Night Creatures	58
Spring Break	59
Decision	60
In Open Fields	61
Noisy Bouncer	62
Largo	63
Old Folks at Home	64
Meditation	65
Untitled	66
Cotton Mouth	67
Secret Passage	68
Beside a Spring	70
I Kicked Up a Tonic Bottle	71
Farmer's Field	72
Big Bang Theory	73

I See the Water Tower from Here	75
'til Tomorrow	76

Not Sure Why

Safety First	79
Peaceful Letting	81
Regret	82
Longhand	83
See Saw	84
Diction	85
Skills	86
The Sacred	87
Human Rights Violation #17,898	88
Organization	89
Memorization	90
Trusty Standby	91
Icon	92
Samuel's Ship	93
Wisdom for the Soul	94
World as Audience	95
Honor and Country	96
Psychobabble	97
Jack and a Candlestick, maybe?	98
A Little Off Duval Street	99
Brenda	100

Morning	102
Mind Succubus	103
Irreligious	104
More News	105
Everything but Jesus	106
Panic Attacks	107
Out My Window	108
Yankee Surfer	109
Poet of Truth is Dead to this World	110
Surprised	111
UNnecessary	112
Shut Out	113
Postmodern Acheever	114
Ribe Tuchus	115
Sprinkling	116
Backyard Bounds	117
Preference	118
Agoraphobia	119
At White Springs	120
Shallows	121
To My Love (Giovanna)	122
Soft Shell Turtles	123
Pure Hearts	124
Waiting After Sunday School	125
Lilith	126
The Stalks	127
Comfortable Moments	128
For Joy Harjo	129

An Altus Wedding	130
Flightline	131
What Really Caught My Attention in *Catcher in the Rye*	132
Tides Past	133
River Flood	134
Little Lamb	135
A Rolling Stone	137

I Suwannee

History

Suwannee -

Suwani

Echoes and wanderings
of the Timucua and the Apalachee --
Guasaca Esqui
River of the Reeds
aquifer-fed   living waters
flowing to the sun –

Narvaez and Desoto's
River of the Deer
Water over Gold

Swanie of Foster
never seen
never felt

Sue-wahn-ey –
river of my childhood
swinging out alone
swimming back
slowly

The current holds me
warms me in its shallow places
a tannic brew
bubbling with artesian wells
cooling me back

Swan-ey (like Johnny)
I Suwannee my mother would yell
have you any sense to tell?

The river flows backward in my mind
homes flooded
roads and trees
the dog   gone

The mud is gray, lovely clay
easily molded
in my weak hands
weak from holding the oars, and blistered

Swanie –
In the low tide and low water times
when the flow creeps slowly
like a lake in gentle wind,
the sturgeon suffers to find a place
among the ancient mudfish,
gar, catfish, alligator

15

It's harder for the soapberry
flat woods plum
the red chokeberry, parsley haw, warblers,
redstarts, bracken, chain, and brake –
The greenfly orchid and
stinky jimson weed
must run deep below the nightshade
with its deadly black berries –

It's harder upon the thick bog hemp
the red-winged blackbird
in the undergrowth with the swamp sparrow
and the marsh rice rat
cooling off with a warm drink
along the shallow shoreline –

The infrequent manatee will be more
infrequent, as searches for vegetation
become harder as its wide body
must traverse along with ski boats –

Close by
mines glow radiant phosphorous white,
economics being different
since the steamboat stopped
paddling through the maze
the wandering malaise
empty spring house echoing –

Circle of pickups
mosh pit cockfights in moonlight
Saturday nights, slobbering in truck beds
under mossy tentacles –

Southern macker moon scares the brave –
Spot light of coon hunters
covers a multitude of sins
down the river, over holey limerock.

Suwannee
in my early days, my eyes began to see –
I have heard the panther's scream
the storm hiding her –
The lark's tune will never sound the same
on this, my river.

A Poem in Bronte's *Agnes Grey and Poems*

Anne Bronte called those woods a bleak place,
yet no other breeze would do, except in the woods
meeting strangers as they passed with unbidden sigh.
How unhappy, poetry without that poetic place,
down by the riverside, over hill and dale,
straddling the straining brook with line and hook
trying to lure that single chain pickerel, or turning
stones which reveal more life than what is apparent.
Oh, give me back my Home
the bedroom window seat, from where I looked upon
the wild cherry, and felt the gentle summer breeze,
with locust song, mockingbird and bluebird singing.
Oh, give me back my Home
Down upon the Suwannee, where old folks sit alone
biding time till their time be no more, except upon that
other, happier shore, hope in faith still stirring.
Oh, give me back my Home
The joys of youth that now depart
will come to cheer my soul again.
Better now in this life. After all, heaven begins on earth,
and my heart is here, resting among the ferns
feeling a part of the larger, greener, plains of youth.

Sustenance

Early morning flies announce their presence
popping the water's tight skin –
Mayflies, swarming, fertile vectors
small, and delicately mating –
Males, with longer tails, bigger eyes,
push their way upward toward the moon –
Nymphs float to surface
drawing strikes up and down the river –
An otter stays put
balancing between rock and current
a hologram shimmering in early light.

Shallow

Drift wood grooves reveal
marks of the river's rage –
water flowing over, under, across –
facial features in the creases
show a round face
head pointed along the crown

Contained

Clay bank, twenty feet high
root ladders with golden silk webs
chipping sparrows test
each wrung for strength,
as the resurrection fern waves goodbye –

On the far bank
dark trees with shallow whisper
call to my barefoot soul
under this real bridge
reached by crossing a sign, marked
Bridge Closed.

A gar skeleton dries in the sun
above the water line
laid out on a flat red stone. A stone
like I've never seen before.

Homecoming

Random as the gull that glides above
away from sea to feed on fresh
water specimens –
a kite, dancing a sarabande, in white chiffon,
gives the air a salty taste

We're here
beside and above the tall reeds
dancing in the wind
near the slow moving black water
listening to its whispers
attending to its changes
hoping it always stays the same

Crossing Place

An old rusty bridge, condemned.
Not for lack of strength.
Its reason has expired.
It's too narrow
so it sits alone near the new bridge, and
picks up the echoes of each crossing.

Strollers soon discover
the old, lovely bridge.
A romantic place
a Sunday, family picnic place
a tourist place
a place for a closer look at the spring house
between the riveted pig-iron angles.

Sailing It Off, Up the Suwannee

dedicated to Paddy MCAloon, Modern day Shakespeare

Cold water like ichors oozes
from the shell wall window
into the tannic brew
baked by sunny days –
The best spot is where they meet
a happy medium of ice and tea.

Down By The River Side

Tiptoeing through hyacinths
a heron hunts for fingerlings
unaware of what lurks
in the shadows cast by morning fog –
Dew drops slide
down the face of a butterfly orchid.
A single pounce
a slamming plunge –
loose feathers float in circles downward
forming a headdress shape in round –
gray, deep, and light blue hues
organized nearly, then scattered.

Fountain of Youth

Cloud scape and moon beam
dusk in autumn air
stillness cottony over black water.
The water, nice, and worthy to drink,
though not as healing as once supposed.
Healing, it is, to sit on a rock, and
catch your breath
beside the moving waters
away from the burgeoning crowd.
Here, smallness is still celebrated,
as well as the grandiose.

The Underground River

sometimes revealed by artesian wells in farmers' fields
small holes beside a pond
sinkholes blocking traffic
an inconspicuous spot in a riverbed.
Sulphur-scented
icy-cold summer pool, and
hot tub in winter.
Sirens slither by way of the moon
milky-eyed,
haunted by bright light.

Day

Panting for air
I did not mean to suck your life away.
It started as a breath
below surface,
my body sinking, dragging,
toes never touching.
You wouldn't release.
You dared to drown,
so that I remained
with the last breath.
My eyes aflutter
my dying wish, to keep your face
locked in my memory
here beneath the setting sun
before night falls again.

Like Searching

for a clear bag in water
deciphering becomes tough
when made to choose.
Had I two choices
I'd struggle to find another way, and
I'd grip the wheel tighter,
look through the windshield
at blustered Highway 90
fearing this Fall may be my last.

The Shoals

long, winding, casual kissing
lapping strakes
wetting the face
in all the right places –
a gardener in wet sod
planting on cool banks
suctioned into gray clay ––
sliding of viscous fluids
between slimy stones
over falling places

Dawn's
also published in *Arden*

misty, sensuous fog
covers her body complete –
light charging her surface
strikes the irises in waking –
my hands full of her
falling from me
down into her own hollow
completely unrestricted
like fire in a dry forest
forever unquenched

Down

Floating h e a r t s spread over the deep,
unafraid of what lurks below
of what buries itself in the mud.
Anchored
uninvited bodies with swollen eyes.
A full history
of lost fish baskets
too deep to hook and retrieve,
full of skeletons
stacked one on top of the other –
fish feeding upon fish, feeding upon fish.

After the Rain

Carrion near a roadside ditch
a tornado escape
filled with hairy bog hemp
slimy salamanders
palmettos, green geisha fans
waving in the wind –
tropical hammock
lottery ball spinning
breezy summer afternoon –
chirps and gargles
dripping pond pines
white peacocks
moved slightly
then still

Deep Tones

The grass is greener in the park –
the carillon plays folk songs
once heard from wooden, hand-built steamers –
Old oak and cypress roots
deeper than the river –
the river runs slow and shallow
like the pulse of a dope fiend
raised only when flooded –
its arteries straining to give life.

Fixed

Cambered branches of elder oak
cambric tendrils spiralling
over tepid, textured ripples
slippery, shelly banks –
cantabilis
capricious chanting
echoed tones cloistered far away
from the clop-clop noise of pig iron
and rubber, over bridges
structured frantically unaware

Tourists

Limestone wall banks make it easy to climb
a poolside ladder
with breaks, cuts, and smooth holes for feet.
If I climb high enough, I can dive back down, and
woo travelers resting in lounge chairs,
cucumbers in their eye sockets
lotion covering their pale shells
yellowing toe nails, varicose veins.

An Old Bridge Pylon

sits like a missile
jammed into the bank
into the sugary white sand
another tall, standing testament –
man can create

Its rusty sediment
releases heavy metal onto the sand
into the water –
a little graffiti would really set it off –
after all,
it's going to be here for a very long time.

The Live Oak

Most of the old grandaddy oaks are gone.
Their weight too much for guide wires
to hold them fast like puppets at the Jardin des Plantes.
The kids today won't see them as I saw them
like giant mushrooms on the horizon.

All I have is memories of the huge arms
wider than a horse's back
holding me fast as I scooted above the pond.
Later I would walk out over the water, no hands,
showing my bravery to a crowd of spectators, and
most follow my lunacy.
I would like to say there will one day be
more of the giant trees,
but instead I must say, "Sorry kids, you shall never
see them, indeed."

Bald Eagles

nest in tall trees
close to the water –
they swoop down, turning at the precise
moment

their bodies glide above the surface
holding that pattern
until their heads are up
thoughts on the sky

they are too calculating
to symbolize a nation –
too elegant and divine
to grace us at all

Formation

Pecan trees in wintery moss and   splotch
stand like gray ghosts on the battlefield.
Their forgotten fruit
litter earth like palmetto   roaches
smashed by heavy foot
from a creaky bough.
Fog hangs
Settling between
their weary
arms
like
silent   death

Out of Water

Let not the water overflow.
Sink me not out in the deep.
I am poor and needy,
lost among my own
ashamed and confounded.
Laid up in shackles of iron
the web cast against me
dark sayings
wicked wanderers –
I, their fool.

Opression destroys the sane
covered in darkness –
black waters
cover my head by inches
the oak above my reach
my soul departs this earth.
Found, in his eyes, without favor –
he who dwells in the garden.
I am a captive, desolate creature
the darkest stains

I can't help but rise up above the water
to meet my soul
fitted before the worlds were breathed.
My Lord divides the sea
my heart
        my blameless heart
        full of the tears of joy.

*When a man's ways please the LORD,
he maketh even his enemies to be at peace
with him.* -- **Proverbs 16:7**

I Am Clay in a Kiln

fired too brittle –
mark me a way from this river of my childhood.
Cut it in stone by the waterway.
Peace shall destroy us all
in this time of the end.
I see things the river has shown me –
blood red skies
diverse ramblings I do not understand.
Many people wandering by the water
washing
yet not becoming clean –
desiring a little dew
to moisten their faces
to stop the burning
felt in their eyes.

Understanding is a wellspring of life unto him who has it: but the instruction of fools is folly.

-- Proverbs 16:22

Horses

stand high out of the mist:
the work of your hands.
They explode forward
pressing the earth firmly,
dancing along the river
in furious flight
kicking up the soft sand.
Their weight snaps roots like twigs
under the thorn tree,
waiting for an order
waiting for your voice.

Bird's Eye View

Foresters usually see smoke before the flames.
That's what they said in the tower on a school trip.
The wind moved the small post about,
even on that clear autumn day.
I wondered what it would be like
to stay in the woods testing trees, and clearing thickets,
plowing wide swathes to keep flames from spreading.
Now I had something besides
a Smokey Bear ad or a striking match.
Practical learning.
The stairs back down made me nauseous
like the tower on the flightline later would
or walking the ladder of a C-5 Galaxy.
Some people just weren't made for lofty spaces.
Some people prefer looking up rather than down,
without any desire to be up away from the ground.

Metamorphosis

With obscured view, and
befuddled flesh
a conscious image of ambition –
it mothers over free-flying conflict
escapes its elongation
transformed to flutter.
Fairy dust of tempted Eve
spread over this physical plane
among countless cousins
in downy meadow

```
          r           t
f              e e           o
```

```
            FLY
```

Off 136A
for Shawn and Bethany

```
The ground here b                       God flow sustaining
                   o                 e
              w                  h
                   s  to the river t
           angered into whirling under

        formed as it rolls          t

past rocks and fallen trees –        o
undertows carry things d
undercurrent          o            w
where they wash a ay  w
released again dow    n   s t r e a m     s
caught and released again and again and again again again again
until no more

          n d
Grou      swells
                        A C
                      V
                      E
                        R N S, b
                              e    a
                                      c  h  e  s
              sinkholes

formed by the        c  u  r  r  e  n  t
a canvas   a medium   an artist
                                 rolling strokes of the brush
```

alllllll daaaaaaay loooooooooong   everyday
It cannot stop creating its art
even if [retained]

as steady and sure as life and death
the river moves –
and when a day is done
it goes on into the next
rolling across the land ^^_

on its unending journey to some other

                                        P l A c E

An Upside Down Umbrella

c   cts rainwater.
o   e
  l l

       a pool

s
t
u
c
k   in the earth

   spinning round on its cap point➤

   The water s o h s –
         l s e

           settled only when the wind
     bre   akes from its horseplay

Degrees of Heat

Yellow –
Cool melon –
Black-eyed susans in the breeze
Cool Spring mornings
Honey combs oozing
Honeysuckle vines
Covering bright shutters

Red –
Cool melon –
Poppies in a field
Hot Summer mornings
Roses covered in dew
Your dress with white polka-dots
Picnic blanket in the shade
I caress you tightly
Sweat beads

Blue –
Propane flame –
Sky without clouds
Deep sea fissures
Klamath calmness
Dowry without reward
Mediterranean sardines
Lips blowing hard on a tenor sax

River Caverns

run for miles
glowing white in darker hours –
Two openings in the bank
each large enough
for an adult person to enter
separated by one foot of rock

Tired of holding my breath
I pant and move my legs back and forth
like I used to do in church
my mother smacking them,
begging me to stop

A log floats by, and
I send it onto a ledge in the bank –
centipedes, millipedes, scorpions, roaches,
a roly-poly, and a daddy long leg spider
run out of the log's many crevices

I take a final breath and plunge myself
down into the ground, beneath the water's surface –
I use the cave ceiling to push myself inside, and
there it opens up, a coliseum with brilliant light
so deep the bottom cannot be found
so beautiful I forget to breathe, and
after a moment of this underground paradise
I turn to find the exit

I re-take my seat upon the clay bank,
breathing deeply
I prepare for another dive, as
my legs shake uncontrollably,
goose bumps up and down my back –
dark soon
crickets in the woods are singing
a song about the river

Johnny Darter Planted in Leafy Mud

water running o'er his head
yet he holds fast
thrilling us as we watch
the jet-black hero
appear and disappear,
bubbles in a brook.
His ancient body, with mud coursing
through transparent veins
camoflaged by clear water
and dirty water, too –
A frog in a bog
laying still like a hen
in dark, shadowy places –
His belly to the rock
the silver-dotted pusher
flexes his pecs

Locals

swing on ropes
out into the middle of the river
their own rebel yells –
Small children swim in the shallows
with pastic boats
beach rakes and shovels
eating crackers from a box –
their mommas holding them.
They run back and forth grabbing crackers
changing toys
blowing noses
crying on momma's shoulder
harming nothing, except
a small niche
set in the branch
by a rope.

Movement

Clover covers the high bank of Swift Creek.
The black water rushes
washing the bottom of the bridge
spraying passers by
as it moves the way geography demands
down its slippery slope to sea –

Its darkness unaffected by daylight
it meanders through farmers' fields
covered by woods
pasted along its shoreline like painted brows
plucked by busy landowners
watching its flow from their breakfast nooks –

Livestock drink from shallow pools
filled with yesterday's rainwater, and
tadpoles, mosquito larvae, cow dung –
naturally occuring phenomena to country folk
a diminishing breed
with the influx of metropolitan seduction.

Flint litters the ground.
Rubbing two pieces to make a spark
damp oak leaves start and sputter
dry moss catches and smokes
feeding tiny flames.

Black bears have been here
leaving their heavy claw marks in the mud
scratching bark from the Live Oak
rooting for earthworms in the hammock bedding
disturbing each and every trash can.
Yet, it's been a while now since I've seen one.

Out of tune, this station –
its receivers need troubleshooting
new solenoids for its actuators –
it's all painted feathers and plastic tom-toms
faux leather skins on hard plastic cans
drumsticks too greasy.

Summer Time

It's quiet here –
It's a summer morning.
The crew chief sits high on the sleigh
shouting orders –
then comes the burning hot sun.
The sun always demands
the tobacco come out before
it burns up on the stalk.
It is in us not to stop until the job is done
not to stop until the day is gone.

By Chance Viewing

A common gray fox scampers through oak leaves
chasing a small animal
never noticing my presence on this big lime stone –
rare, sighting a fox after day break,
they're always in my headlights
dashing for the woods,
eyes, glowing road flares.

This one wants its prey,
so badly it bangs its head against a tree.
Shaking its head side to side due to the impact
it finally sees me below, staring
yet doesn't move
as if the impact has done something to its eyes.

Then it slowly walks away
the way domestic animals do –
its bushy tail bouncing back and forth
a pom-pom or wall duster
pointing to the sky
to the hidden stars.

Night Creatures

Nocturnal animals are mysterious –
like the scream of a panther in the back yard.
In the morning, tracks deep in the ground
filled in by early morning rain.
Tree marks –
deep etches – deeper than natural.

The lake, dried up, tall grass.
A shame, the way it happens
a prairie, in place of wetlands,
the water over-used for farming, and then
made habitable for retirees
tired of freezing rain.

Giant alligators once bellowed under the stars
right where I stand in this sandy depression
once covered in water plants --
I've left fishing string near this shore line, and
bothered nests,
scattered eggs, like marbles, across the sand.

Spring Break

She cut chicken silhouettes from feed bags,
sitting in her lawn chair,
her beautiful Cherokee skin contrasting
the yellow nylon straps.
Red roosters as faded as her memory of the asylum.

A photo in a cheap, ragged frame
shows eight children of comparable ages, and a
beautiful but tired mother –
also a gray-haired father, near the wood stack
holding a guilty pose.

Silhouettes chase each other
close to where she had them hidden –
her frail legs, her sturdy frame, weary.
The film in the Super 8 projector
switches over
to another part of my childhood.

Decision

A mockingbird
bounces up and down on the boxwoods
upset her eggs are threatened
by a black snake
moving along the trellis.
Should I smash its head,
deprive it, or
let it eat the eggs –
Something in the mother's cry
moves me to move the aggressor
as it slithers downward
forked tongue honing in on its meal
eager to swallow.

It strikes.
I hold it back with a cane.
Forgive its transgression
sure it's unaware of my power
to let it live or die –
sure of its instinct
not to know the difference
when it comes to us.

In Open Fields

cypress trees draw lightning.
Their knees make good door stops.
Beautiful brown hues
the nicest wood –
white egrets sit in branches
making cackling noises,
a black
rain-filled sky behind them.

After a good rain
the marsh runs over, sending water
across the pasture and into the road, and
into a pond with no name.

Water
less than a foot deep
collects across the field.
So many fish to be gathered.
So many
flopping about
looking for deeper water.

Noisy Bouncer

Young crow ululations
break sweet sparrow song –
the smartest of all fowl,
perhaps from talking so much, or
stealing smarts from the dove.
Not so rare as the crafty raven
they hop about in fields of hay
cawing up bugs
hidden like needles
along broken fence line.

Largo

The oak and its roots are gone.
The woods cleared for a mobile home.
The lush field, now only a vacant lot.
Any other street corner in the world
exactly the same.

Yet, the pond, still there
keeps our secrets in its reflections
springing with life
regardless of what happens beside.

Old Folks At Home

grind sugar cane to make dark cane syrup
so sweet a spoon-full will do the trick.
The grinder, powered by a mule
attached to a swinging arm.
Dad slices peels from a stalk
giving me and my brothers a taste.

Slicing across the break
a black racer
crossing countless rows of cane
searching in all four directions.

Meditation

Flying squirrels fall at night.
Green bottle flies find them warm.
The porch, invisible,
evening sky, dim moonlight.
A pack of dogs howl in the bog
where rabbit-sized rats roam,
tunneling in and out of the hog yard.
A polyphemus moth lands on the screen
looking in, as we sit just a talkin'
rocking on wood rockers
amazed by its span, suspended in open air.

Untitled

Tying a mayfly at a family lake
giant green gowns spread out
lonely without their dancers.
Operatic players cover the stage
singing to their spectators –
a fat baritone pumps up the crowd
echoing a wake of vibration
clear across to where I sit
anticipating a marvelous show.

Cotton Mouth

sits invited
in an ancient cypress,
heel's deadly enemy
hides its head –
as the boat drifts closer
the turban
loosens its grip.

Secret Passage

The Suwannee starts at the Okefenokee –
the Alapaha, Withlacoochee, and Santa Fe,
fill the Suwannee
on its course to the Gulf of Mexico
widening all along the way –
first the distance of a short rock toss,
then a mile.

At Sandy Point, we'd embark on journeys
up along the Santa Fe to the Itchetucknee
where the moonshine-clear water mixes with the dark –
we swam and trapped crawdads
using the boat to dry off.

Then we traveled back down the Santa Fe
to where it opens up
swallowed by the Suwannee
so wide, the distant shore blurred in the hot sun.
Dad opened up the throttle
hair whipped, pasted to our heads.

There, along the river, a passage to a spring
assessable only by boat
a scene like *Creature from the Black Lagoon* –

narrow passes, low-hanging moss and limbs –
clear water

We didn't know most of the people
so we swam and listened to talk
wondering about their secret speech
laughter and body language.

We wandered the woods
dug mastodon teeth from ancient mud pits
held our breath under the chilly spring water
ignoring the confusion of the adult world.

Beside a Spring

Crystal surface and nectar well
bee on knees in peanut shell
yellow, piled pollen,
lines and guarded swell,
hollow, angled stem,
old plant roots and woody smell –
soil to grasp and blossom ripe
centered bolls and shiny bell

I Kicked Up a Tonic Bottle

covered in mud and leaves
made of depression-era glass,
its stopper half-destroyed,
it had no contents

I tried to smash it against a tree
several times before it's lost –
Perhaps a wanderer through
these woods will find
a baby blue bottle
clean it up for display
enjoy its imperfect molding

Farmer's Field

A cow skull, upright in a row of pines.
Sounds heard, herd unwatched,
hoofing the tree line, chewing the cud,
oodles of flies incite forward movement.
Small initiates
steadier on their feet than hours ago
struggle up the knoll.

Appliances and old crates,
wood scraps and dilapidated furniture
fill a hole in the ground.
Soggy old clothes beside
a nearby pond, known for its gator,
muddy water, with an unknown depth.

Big Bang Theory

       The Oort cloud made it
happen.   Wheeling motions
                 solar flare
       Ezekiel's chariots of fire
         rising high
      and coal burning d

                             e

                             e

                             p

inside the   ey ^ es
                the creatures inside the wheels
     my fibers striating like cotton
         on the gin, over the
rocks, and a green bottle
        Bright Lights
         I think

Big Bang

Impossible as Aphrodite –
   I like big bangs, though –

      Rockets   and

         jets

         m
         is
         si
         le

I think of NASA
    Tang in the morning, and
               water mills
Don Quixote with his legs
          bound by hemp rope
   The Oort cloud s
                w
       n   i
  g   i   r
     l

            around him, with

   Helios   and   Aeolus

I See the Water Tower from Here

An old black man sips from his brown bag
eating honey buns with sardines, sopping the oil –
He don't mind if I watch –
I've talked to him down by the river
he fishes three lines
some kind of sorghum bait

Bugs buzz all around the ball field lights, and
I concentrate on them
they calm me on the mound –
I always blow up by the third or fourth inning –
Attention deficit, they'd say today

The rhythm of MoTown thumps in cars passing
as young girls dance to the beat
up on the top bleacher, behind the plate –
Over in the park
a merry-go-round spins on its own, as
older playground toys rust under large oaks
echoes of raquetballs ringing

'till Tomorrow

Water sounds and daylight fades
nightingales in sallowy shades
fly about like fits of rage
happied by the close of day –
The silvery sand a constant place
to watch them chase the lost light's face

Not Sure Why

Safety First

I told my Ukrainian friend, a missionary,
he'd better strap his son into the seatbelt,
safety in this way not so understood by Europeans.
I remember my Italian father-in-law
the first time I drew a fist, angered by not readily finding
my seatbelt in his Fiat Uno
at the airport in the very hot August of '88, and
August not a month Sicilians like to be caught outside, let alone
caught outside for four hours, waiting
for the late aircraft carrying a mystery son-in-law from another land –
My missionary friend's young lad, fragile from travel and from being
a missionary's son from Ukraine,
worried me, as I thought he wouldn't survive the impact
as we hit Atlanta traffic around 4:30 PM –
But we made it to the bus station, and on time, yet
his wife seemed a little nervous about the crowd of people at the depot,
but I had to get on to Birmingham to pick up my own wife,
who would incidentally
be late anyway.
My friend's wife told me her husband had gone to the bathroom as I
walked up from behind her, returning from my supposed departure –
I smiled and handed her some sandals for her husband,
sandals my brother had given to me the day before
but I would never wear them
they're too narrow –

As I drove off I thought about the atrocities
acted upon the Eastern Europeans during the big wars
and some for loving Jesus –
special hate, like that of Stalin, re-emerges
now and again and reminds us who it is we serve.

Peaceful Letting

My hard drive crashed again, and
this time I lost 60 pages of a poetry manuscript, a novel
written on for over two years, and over one hundred family pictures –
it's okay though
I tell myself –
in my stoic mind I tell myself that the work was too easy, way
too easy to be upset over, and
it's true, as I never shed a single drop of blood
over the electrons formed into letters
on a screen of white, and
no one died to get it right, and
no mobs had formed outside my place
to keep me from writing those words
glowing at night as I sat eating cheesecake while
watching something mildly entertaining on TV –
The way I see it, the poems must have been bad, or
I would have made sure to get my new Apple before now –
if they had deserved an Apple, they would still be with me.

Regret

It was not by chance,
the woman had lived a very carnal and vicious life, and
of course, no one had expected her to tarry
quite so long with us,
but for some reason her death still shocked me.
The dog seemed to keep its distance, and
her kids looked pale, having vanilla ice cream
from a pail on the stoop,
and there it was that I worried about the inevitable,
though myself a believer,
with plenty of promise and hope for a future in my Savior
post earth
yet that was not it at all, as I sat
about to cry over her, dead to us in every conceivable way

Longhand

Oh, the rote skill of handling a keyboard –
it would be a crime to consider keyboarding at the same time
as the gentle manner involved in creating perfect space between
letters in front of a class and under pressure, at the board.
It's mostly gone forever, like the giant oak trees.

See Saw

Remember the meanies who would abandoned
the teeter totter just as you'd reached
the zenith of experience,
your head just below the elm branch, and
oh the pain in the rump to be driven down to earth
just as you had closed your eyes in
the ecstasy of being airborne?
Yet, you'd do the same to someone else that same week
from weakness and for revenge perhaps, and
perhaps that's why the name changed to seesaw, since
it became a game of "Did you see what Davey
did to Chuck?" with the response of,
"Oh, I saw it, but I really got Joey last week."

Diction

Ever notice how so many phrases are not really meant
for poetry?
Words like menstrual cramps, pin worms, pipe insulation,
power steering, pressure cooking, extension cord, eyebrows,
larding, laryngitis, or rubbings and skunk odor –
"I declare Isabelle, did you hear what that man just read
in his poetry?"
No, it is strange enough to use bubonic plague, hysterectomy,
globules, piddling pickets, jabbering misfits,
or unstoppable mouths.

Skills

I just earned the title of tutor, online –
I passed all seven exams that certify me
to do what I went to school to do,
and what I have done for ten years of my life –
what if I had failed those exams after bragging
about how good I was on my cv, at what
it is that I do?
I guess I would have withered up and died
right inside the flower bed of my drive
where all the other dogs go to urinate

The Sacred

As a Southern poet who often writes of nature,
I guess I ought to mention:

m o c k i n g b i r d s

"Marvel not, my brethren, if the world hate you." -- 1 John 3:13

Human Rights Violation #17,898

I just finished reading an article about the Chinese government bulldozing Christian churches over,
eradicating any sign that the heartless Christ followers
ever existed in their beautiful countryside,
out of their precious sight, their eyes wide open now,
too open to warrant another butting in,
another reminder of sin

Organization

The label on my file basket reads, "This Week's Stuff,"
and it's been overflowing for months –
I'm not sure when I let it go –
it's filled with broken headsets, money bags,
boxes of envelopes,
unaskedfor magazines
unfilled plastic binders, business cards,
Frogtape with PaintBlock,
my wallet {Hey! My wallet!}
some electric cord for something
labels meant for other baskets, and
a sign that reads, "Make Checks Payable To …"

Memorization

Ever played with hand shadows against
a wall in a new place
with a lamp with no shade
during winter in a strange land, and
you couldn't remember the goat and pig,
but the hare and donkey
came as easy as snow falling on stoops in darkness?

Trusty Standby

The easiest of hand shadows is the duck
for all you need is an okay sign
and fingers spread till stuck

Icon

Ever wanted to fly that rocket,
the symbol for Launchpad on your Apple?
It's like the little cartoon ones from old TV shows,
back when becoming an astronaut was actually
more of a possibility,
with Tang stuck on my spoon and on the roof of my mouth –
well, maybe not my dream –
somebody's dream

Samuel's Ship

Mississippi steam boats could handle
the treachery of the swooning spring,
yet could be held by a string, while
people flowed on and off with their packets, and other supplies
and sundries, and I assume,
they traveled comfortably, or wouldn't have traveled –
the ships changing their courses like corsets,
the delta as unpredictable as a poem, and
somewhere among them, Captain Clemens.

"With the ancient is wisdom; and in length of days understanding." -- **Job 12:12**

Wisdom for the Soul

The information super highway has changed society more toward the bad, I feel,
mostly because everyone's suddenly wise.
But wisdom is a slow pot that simmers for years,
and holds to tested and tried philosophies, and from there, builds –
the kind of stuff the average web surfer avoids like ebola.

World as Audience

"In the beginning God created the heavens and the earth."
This memory verse card in my office
reminds me that my creation of poetry could be
as beautiful as life itself,
and filled with the splendor of all the colors in the palette,
and yet I could still be sent off down the road,
my poems scattered along the alleyways,
out into the rain gutters,
littering up the highways of Alabama.

Honor and Country

dedicated with love to my Uncle Ronald Boyce Brown, or Rocky

A Mr. Adkins finally got his Medal of Honor, and they
showed everyone on television news the event, and
the look on his face, a little odd,
sort of like the look I used to make at school
when pushed around -
so cute for an old guy,
in his nice uniform
they certainly must have provided
after all of these years of waiting –
I think of my Uncle Rocky
with his seizures due to shrapnel, and
the murderous screaming at night
the fighting with my mother
the bodily smells that emanated from his corpse
as he sat on our couch and played it cool
like everything was just fine,
his innumerable bottles of pills in paper sacks
all around the house,
his demons flying from room to room, cutting
through the smoke and malfeasance,
finding some way to escape his presence.
But now he finally rests,
fully expecting Jesus to give him love,
and He does – He does.

Psychobabble

Some book I picked up on dreams,
this evening at my daughter's,
read that if I dreamt of gaiters
I should expect to celebrate gaily or be filled
with amusement.
I thought, "What are gaiters?"
Kinda hard to dream of something I never knew existed.
So I tried to dream of this mystery gaiter,
as I closed my eyes in her kitchen,
but all I could think of was volleyball –
I'd rather watch glue dry than watch volleyball –
Or perhaps a gaiter is what I have always dreamt of
but have never known.

What a crock!

Jack and a Candlestick, maybe?

Remember the poem with a similar name
about a Jack,
and in my version
he's jumping flames on sticks, or maybe he
bounces balls between jacks and pick up sticks,
trying to get to the nimble and the quick
while feeling awfully sick.
Or maybe Jack's coming down
driving those jacks
deep inside his plantar artery —
Jack-o-Lanterns light up like his face, foot in pain,
or maybe he's a lost boy jacking cars
on freeways on Sunday mornings,
leaving emergency crews to pry
.40 cal hollows from backs
with jack sticks
bloody baseball bats
hidden behind bellicose
bench seats covered in faux fur.

A Little Off Duval Street

Rawhide laces
over and underhand,
knots,
two cuts
top grain, shaped square,
baseball tied, the best with more stitch –
practice game, tied,
then, down under bright lights, with the energy
of onlookers,
tight games kept close, and
hanging on the dugout chainlinks,
the worn, strung out gloves

Brenda
dedicated to my Mother

Brenda macrame'd plant holders
for native Florida varieties, hung
fit in the yard –
She tanned belts and stamped designs,
taught cubs, crafts mostly,
Wednesdays, after school –
She kept books, sold Avon, worked as secretary,
washed our clothes and hung them
on aluminum strands between T shaped poles –
We helped her clean top to bottom, Saturdays –
I liked to help her shop in our big brown van,
with shag carpet, huge windows, a fridge, pilot seats, and
crappy stereo.
She asked once
if I thought she were beautiful,
and I said yes, without having to lie –
She cooked big stews, and slopped me and my brothers without
getting her fingers bitten.
She fished, a lot, and played softball, a lot,
and won a golf trophy once, for the longest drive –
She danced disco, out drank my dad, and
had a laugh that would raise a roof –
She sat with me at 3am when I got the croup,
and I woke the neighborhood.

She kept her mother
after the hospital stays, the accusations, and
she helped her brothers
find their way through the abyss, and listened
as her sisters shared stories of the wrong men, and
explained how perfect hers was, and
she helped the Murats across the street in their final days
clean and cut grass and pull weeds, and hope for better
than all the pain death brings along with it, and
I see her hands now, chapped and healing from incisions
to remove cancerous cells,
and I am so glad to have these memories, and
to know mom's closer to Jesus than ever.

Morning

Sometimes, I feel like opening a window
to make shrieking sounds, like in Sicily,
yelling back at vendors
yelling up to the balconies
for their regulars
to get them to come out to buy eggs, greens, garlic,
and sometimes fruits, like small melons, lemons, figs –
I sit watching,
learning Sicilian language not found in books
even on Sicilian language,
though most of these *venditore*
wouldn't have an education past fifth grade,
some with teeth missing, old clothes worn over and over,
though clean and neat,
they remind me of what America used to be, and
in some small ways, how I wish it still was

Mind Succubus

Awakened again in this red chair,
hands and feet with stigmata
the same stale air –
I don't wanna
get up, and I don't care, and
something has to change,
or something oughta!

"Jesus said, 'For judgment I have come into this world, so that the blind will see and those who see will become blind.'" -- **John 9:39**

Irreligious

An article on the 'Internet' states Pope Francis
decrees he will give blessings
allowing people out of purgatory, early, if followers
will tweet with the Vatican –
Sordid religiosity, if it's at all true, and remember
Jesus turned the tables, so
what might His tweet policy be?

More News

A certain Russian industry leader gives
a priest a jet airplane, so
this will surely raise the stakes
here in America. I mean,
all televangelists will be wanting tax advantages
for new fighter jets:
"Pontif plows missiles into the West Bank this morning,
trying to out do fundamentalists
still uneducated about all the bells and whistles
offered by their craft."

Everything But Jesus

The dates of the Shang Dynasty
confirm that the Bible is accurate about all of us
coming from the Mesopotamian Valley, and
they've found a gigantic rock
like a mountain in the promised
land, an altar place called, Sin.
And though they say they've found Sinai,
I wonder if Sin is short for Sinai, but they didn't
rub quite hard enough to reveal its full name?
Maybe this is the reason Christ will split
the Mt. of Olives in two, since he's already dealt with sin?

Panic Attacks

My wife had them years ago, and
now my college-aged daughter follows suit
shivering in warm clothes on a Wednesday night
after sitting for a Chinese couple
preparing for their dissertations and defenses –
everyone on the block so stressed
trying to get somewhere
an arrival won't even matter in a decade,
or two from now –
My wife yells how she just has to handle it
like she also had to,
no reason to pussy foot around with these things,
it will only make it worse.
My daughter asks for her baby sister instead, and
after a bout of moving about on the patio,
then back inside for some Chinese tea,
my daughter wants me to drive her back home
where she must work on a project
due first thing in the morning.

Out My Window

Hollers come as a driver in a van
drags a man by his shirttail
caught in the automatic door
in the cool of a Fall day –

I thought the world had come to an end
and on such a still morning
dry, no rain, and in a month the garden will be starting
to give up its last
for lack of water and sun

But she stopped before he fell
she gave him a chance to catch his stride
to stand upright –

Yet the monarchs kneel much longer now,
their natural photovotaics working overtime
to warm them enough for flight,
but I don't think they will make it –
the ones that lift a little
do not crash land
but die slowly on the new compost

Yankee Surfer

A native Floridian
Combs the beach with his chubby toes,
Envious of a Yank geri-surfer
With taut skin, tan bod, and
  Serious shorts –
This Yank paddles through breaks
Like a Navy Seal, and
Swings his body
Where his butt's
 To the board, and
    Then he turns and pushes and places himself
   Onto his feet –
  He

```
            J
          I
        G
      S        right, and he


        J
          A
            G
Facing the native on        S   left
  the beach                       he rides his tube
    as tubular as               they get, for Florida – the
```
sun's early eastern rays highlight the surfer's fearlessness –
  The chubby Florida Cracker on the beach winces his toes as they
cramp in wet sand - his belly aches for fried oysters
on a Poor Boy sandwich
with hot sauce.

Poet of Truth is Dead to this World

Truss me
across the divide
walk on me
to the other side

Flicker at me
you flighty and flimsy models
look on me
for the remainder of the totals

Soak me
partisan of a meaning
in a sticky burden
hard worker seeming

Conspire against me
contract a new desire
flawless in your planning
serried little liar

Separate me
with a sermon steeped in sleekness
twiddle those bargaining chips
reveal truculent weakness

Utter me
pundit for the puffed up
gauge the gaping galaxy
execute and conduct

Surprised

The chimes of the Sicilian church scare me
with my winding path
afraid of the alleyways of life
no medal for courage
no scars on my face
my folding cart filled with worthless rocks –
Priscilla at the schoolhouse
dribbles a ball past with her dirty shoes
her feet level with the top of my head –
I see them all wearing plastic shoes
from Taiwan or China,
a shame, with a cobbler on this very block
ready to make real shoes –
I'd go hungry a month to have decent shoes
out on that unforgiving turf –
hunger pangs of the advantaged
or weak, or mean,
in a world where to be,
requires a dowry.

UN necessary

Before combustion engines hurled past
with oiled mechanisms,
tiny hummingbirds congregated
under the eaves
late in the afternoon, as cicadas
began tuning up
for an evening of sonatas

Before fiber optics,
eyes pierced past window sills and
set a course of wild imaginings
scaped by cultured minds, creating
plotted fancies fit for a lord, and
stone laid upon stone
the only walls that girdled sight
save for mountains
which rose above all who desired to be

Bowels, in pain and twisted
push up the foulness
into blood-shot eyes
watchers communicate across nations
yet, who plants this vineyard
in dangerous global sunlight
this bad seed, and
the men and women in blue uniforms
refuse honorable seppuku

"When I am afraid, I put my trust in you." -- **Psalm 56:3**

Shut Out

Do you function?
I take it you're fine, regardless of
my culpable nature, and
borne personal crosses –
My complete
love for despair, though,
bothers me, and
my usual way of listing –
Death all around me, and
the notes tacked to doors
weigh like stones,
brook stones
concrete shoes –
The current's
surface, my door,
and once I get down beneath,
my worries wash away like God promises
each morning.

Postmodern Acheever

Metrosexual man
where's the Porterhouse? did the Delmonico have to go?
picking your teeth too nasty for you?
why so many Jupiters?
you like trying on patterns, and
sizes ... she likes various sizes
she's been taught to choose well, the tigress
with her late night meetings and dinners with Japanese
techno types cornering the market shares, and
before you know it, wifey's had her fill
before the late night train to Poughkeepsie, and
for you, tomorrow, a new day, and
paisleys are back in style
along with bell bottoms

Ribe Tuchus

A writer's deck card stuck to my wall,
as art, reads *ribe tuchus*,
meaning 'to sit still,' or so it says below the phrase –
I begin to wonder how often I do 'sit still' –
Buffalo in Oklahoma stand still
for what seems like hours
the red rocks near the Red River
rises above the plain
the sound of the rushing brook below me
and in dead stillness the buffalo feels
the need to be still
almost as if pondering the water's movements
magical waters weaving through rounded boulders –
maybe the way a harbor boat sits in the afternoon
after trawling all morning, only catching grunt fish
in a worn out bay, so overworked –
Some say there's too much sitting, and
they say it isn't good for the heart, resting,
yet for most
the stirring seems to start
well before Christmas, and
settles after the first bill arrives in the mailbox.

Sprinkling

Dirt roads in Florida are good when it sprinkles rain
four o'clocks shimmer like silver studs, and
if it's going to storm, it does so earlier than four
stays all day like an uninvited relative.
Thunder before noon, shower till four, or longer.

Indoors by the screen window we'd wait
praying the ball fields could hold their water –
we knew the point of no return
we could pin-point the moment Coach Peppers would call.

The days we wanted to play
were the ones which usually got the most rain, and
faking like you didn't want to play never worked.
I tried it more than once, and ended up making mud balls.
I'd pitch them at the brick wall with great accuracy.

Backyard Bounds

Mom's from a family of eight children –
each embrace tells of her loneliness.

Her four boys woke early
kicking balls between boundaries.

They smashed plants she had to reset
knocking down sheets she'd have to hang back.

New boundaries were set
the game took on new rules.

Else mother would break down
in the sun's sweltering heat.

Hot metal wires held things up
tight between T shaped poles –

Hot metal poles, holding things up
until they had time to dry.

Preference

I prefer to write in this canopy with the yellow meadow
beauty, and its cousin pale, the Brazilian Elodea, seed box,
primrose, white bushy aster, and its cousin
the climber

Better than licking stamps in an air-conditioned office,
though it'd be nice to get a brown bag from the Lantern, and
easy it would be to hang out with the smokers,
watching their toes
grow in their flip-flops

After games dad took us to the Smiley Burger
[when that was a thing], and we'd eat them on the deck, and
it tasted better than prime rib would to me later on
and the stars always lonely

Mornings, early and dark and cold, even in North Florida,
in August, especially in the back of somebody else's pick up
going to somebody else's field to move irrigation pipe
before bringing tobacco in out of the fields

Agoraphobia

A walk in an open field
found deep in the woods –
animals people things
under cover
raising my pulse.

The sway of the tree tops
calms me –
mesmerizes even –

I drive to find the open areas
hidden inside the trees
untouched and wild
scaring a smile onto my face.

At White Springs

The river has breached the springhouse
turning the clear water
a tint of brown –
stagnant stench
no movement at all

dead still.

Shallows

Crawdads hide under loose rock
eels swim in green algae
where the Withlacoochee ends
at the Suwannee

Baby catfish gyrate
amongst the minnows
scattered shadows of laurel oak

Dead leaves cover the bottom
yellow leaf moves in slow current
gray clay between my toes
fishing line broken, forgotten

Holding a ball of clay
I mold a shape
the likeness of a face
then a vessel for drink
a serpent without eyes
back into a ball

I toss it across the river
pick up more clay
fishing will be there tomorrow

To My Love (Giovanna)

you never knew when we started
paper shell pecans were hard to shell
moonshine still boiled at midnight
rabbits were hunted for their feet

you never knew when we started
Southern folks murdered English worse than Italians
yet speak outside for hours, like Italians
talking bad about their neighbors

you never knew when we started
most my meals were tossed to the center of the table
wine came in screw top bottles
peanuts ever existed
there were so many kinds of greens

you never knew when we started
the baggage I carried
the fears I covered up
the stories which I kept inside
yet you continue to believe

Soft Shell Turtles

grow to be massive creatures –
I see them three feet wide with great regularity
hog noses above the water before their shells
they suck the air like a vacuum
suddenly present

I figure the alligators that eat them must be big –
I read about a twenty foot gator once
took seven men to land it –
makes a ten foot johnny boat seem very small
as I stand along the center
pushing my way through a bog

Pure Hearts

I could live here forever
beside the water, as close as humanly possible
to being aquatic
sharing natural existence with God's creatures
which know me
about my sad separation
my tears of guilt
and His blood under nails
hair matted into skin
mud under the eyes –
they feel my fear
and keep safe distance in case
just in case my mind twists
forgetting about grace
forgetting about love

Waiting after Sunday School

for a ride from mom or dad
my thoughts flash from red
to white from red to black
and back off the track
like the rain that hits the pavement
and streams off into grass
downward - earthward

Lilith

Wandering outside time's garden
show your face
prove your existence, as
everything requires proof –

The red devil
tempted Eve, and Adam too,
so what of you?
Are you better than Adam?
Why did you fly away
if you knew how to handle sin?

Show us your face, us
waiting here on asphalt
believing in Christ alone –
prove to us your perfection
us who require a picture.

The Stalks

my answer
to the questions about God –
age old questions of existence, and
they tell me plenty of truth
without argument
pure reason
rising upward toward the sun –
Set them in line
prop them if they lean
see that they are watered and fed
harvest their fruit
turn them under at the appropriate time
where they nourish countless organisms –
fruit innumerable
both in taste and variety
there to enjoy
to store up
give away
transform –
its source, the seed
exists
and had to exist even to be altered
by what they call pure science

Comfortable Moments

Drag yourself back and change the makeup
and go and sin no more
no more
could be possible really
could
be

I need a sabbath of the mind
a day of no thought
time to forget all
a hope to catch up
from all that draws dislocation
the fret or the cause
trips and falls
to a place without chatter
when the mind is scattered
and the order seems too tall –
a restart

For Joy Harjo

The river's steady churn rotates –
a mill carrying debris to the grindstone
deep below the visible

automobiles pass on the bridge above
breaking the steady tempo, or
ebb and flow

no one can see me
hiding behind a concrete pylon
which breaks December wind

the trees have lost their leaves again
the fish their summer appetites
rising to catch warmth

an otter pops up his baby head
a carillon signals noon day
hermetical messages in rhythm

An Altus Wedding

My mockingbirds replaced by Oklahoma roadrunners
black widows by tarantulas
Southern girlfriends by my Southern Italian wife –
we walk boulders
holding hands where the buffalo herd
we wet our feet
making our plans for tomorrow –
we met yesterday
in the hot Sicilian sun
now this tiny Air Force town
waits our return
a reunion –
a stay at the lodge –
where we began, a place to remember
important to abandon

Flightline

sinking sand on this Red River bend, and
I'm as non-native as the natives
searching for my oasis
in this arid stretch of dry bones
with the awful smell of dead carcasses, and
pools of muddy soup
the smell of JP4
the nauseating stretch
across the back of six Galaxies
running full throttle
blowing my hair
my mind
making me sick to my stomach
making me dream of escape
poetry being birthed
my mind writhing in pain

What Really Caught My Attention in *Catcher in the Rye*

catcher in the rye
curves his arms
tightens his stomach
takes his stance
shoulder width apart
knees slightly bent

he knows he's unable
to catch them as they're sent
he drops to his knees
cries in the sand
lifts back again
catching all he can

catcher in the rye
hears the thunderous cries
pounds the hot sand
grains sift through his hands
he drops down again
doing what he can

Tides Past

under red moons
pale moons
yellow moons
bright white neon moons
fiddlers played eagerly
unafraid of malicious fowl, and
fish walked and talked on dry land
in pin-striped suits
with canes and tophats –

Today though, fiddlers scatter off to tiny holes
and fish to deep dark waters
down inside the recesses
where sunken barges lay
slowly rusting away –

so I sneak up on the fiddlers
push them onto my hook
cast them to the deep
where I coax the fish from their safety
dressed only in their scales
their whiskers neatly groomed
gentlemanly smiles
searching for their suits

River Flood

a nightmare anticipated
joy flies by unannounced
a crow, belly tight with corn
a woodland ghost
bell upon the neck
shouting curses
a demon blaming everyone
and there's screaming by the roadside
begging saving grace
desire to know God
in the throat
down the spine
in the feet
as touched
the Spirit flows
healing pain
returning dry land

Little Lamb

(for my old friend Randy Lamb)

Midnight oil is burning
in the churchhouse down the block
the rest of town is sleeping
and I'm sure that they won't stop
bass player could be a blues man
but chose to pick songs for the flock
they say he's casted demons
and they tell me he won't stop

All the girls were deputantes
so I never met them square
they had their fun with all the boys
and loved to tease their hair
sang contemporary songs for Jesus
as they covered their legs with Nair
safe behind the choir loft
I helped the preacher stare

Exchanging secret messages
with the Baptists near the door
I was elbowed by the tenor
just before he hit the floor
it's not we don't love Jesus
the preacher's just a bore
the midnight oil is burning
and it's gonna burn some more

The bass man took a new gig
at the church on down the road
invited me to a party there
said I would not, then I showed
a Valentine's sweetheart banquet
with chocolate cake a la mode
we were asked to write our sweethearts
I wrote to Jesus and stole the show

Midnight oil is burning
in the church house down the block
the rest of town is sleeping
and I'm sure that they won't stop
bass player could be a blues man
but he decided to lead the flock
he's seen his share of demons
in this here one train stop

Midnight oil is burning
I know that it won't stop
bass player pulls all nighters
the lamps never lose a drop
so if you come near our town
and want Jesus as your friend
ask for the bass playing pastor
he'll tell you how Jesus saves from sin.

A Rolling Stone

(also published in *Arden,* but has changed some)

gathers no boss
so take a swim, rock,
in a babbling brook
on the continental rift –
melt into magma
ooze down Roman acquaducts
past Hannibal's legions
past the Tiber
bounce over the Dolomites
crawl up the Alps
fill the holes in the Swiss's cheese
play like you are frozen in Zurich
a duck over you
warming your topside –
grind your compounds into drugs
save a little for yourself
replace bowling balls
then go on strike

www.ingramcontent.com/pod-product-compliance
Lightning Source LLC
Chambersburg PA
CBHW031137090426
42738CB00008B/1124